nickelodeon

JoJo Siwa™

DANCE DREAMS

BuzzPop

Out of this World!

BuzzPop

An imprint of Bonnier Publishing USA
251 Park Avenue South, New York, NY 10010
Copyright © 2018 by Viacom International Inc.
Nickelodeon and all related titles and logos are trademarks
of Viacom International Inc.
JoJo Siwa is a trademark of JoJo Siwa Entertainment, LLC.
Text by Aubre Andrus
All rights reserved, including the right of reproduction in
whole or in part in any form.
BuzzPop is a trademark of Bonnier Publishing USA, and
associated colophon is a trademark of Bonnier Publishing USA.
Manufactured in China TPL 0618
First Edition

1 3 5 7 9 10 8 6 4 2

ISBN 978-1-4998-0837-7

buzzpopbooks.com
bonnierpublishingusa.com

DANCE WORDS

Before you hit the dance floor, unscramble these popular dance terms.

RAHRYHEPCOOG [ ]

LELABT [ ]

ZAZJ [Jazz]

PAT [tap]

ORMNDE [ ]

PO-HPHI [Hip-hop]

LALMBORO [ ]

LOOS [solo]

CRALILY [ ]

SMICU [ ]

See answers on page 31.

Dream Performance

Imagine you're staging the ultimate dance performance for you and your besties. Dream up an event that will get an audience on their feet.

MUSIC

Decide what kind of jams you'll be moving to.

A pop song with a strong beat ♥

A live band with an electric guitarist ♥

An orchestra ♥

A slow, emotional song with great lyrics ♥

Other: ....
....
....
....

LOCATION

Choose the perfect place to perform your masterpiece.

The middle of a busy city square ♡

Onstage in a beautiful theater ♡

At your school's gym ♡

The mall food court ♡

Other: ....
....
....
....

COSTUMES

What will you and your dancers wear?

Colorful costumes that are easy to move in ♡

School uniforms ♡

Anything we want ♡

Sparkly leotards with shimmering tutus ♡

Other: .....DreSS with Beaties.....
.....for the Boys.....
....
....

IF YOUR DANCE IS BEING PERFORMED BY A FLASH MOB, YOU'LL WANT THE DANCERS TO BLEND INTO THE CROWD.

IMPORTANT JOBS

Who will fill these important roles in your performance?

Choreographer (creates the dance routine)

....

Hair and makeup artists (polish everyone's final looks)

....

Wardrobe designer (makes sure everyone's costumes look great)

....

Videographer (records the performance so you can share it!)

....

TAKE 5

Add some chill to your busy day. Color the letters and images while you dream big.

EAT DANCE SLEEP

STRIKE A POSE

JoJo's definitely not afraid of the spotlight. Complete the dot-to-dot to see which pose she's striking.

See answer on page 31.

DANCER GALLERY

Fill this gallery with your Dream Dance Squad.
Tape photos or doodle your own images. Don't
forget to add JoJo!

Glitter

MAKE EVERYONE IN YOUR SQUAD FEEL SPECIAL. GIVE EACH ONE A NICE NICKNAME!

MUSICAL NOTES

Count the musical notes below.
How many of each kind are there?

DID YOU KNOW DANCING A CAPPELLA IS DANCING WITHOUT MUSIC?

See answers on page 31.

Secret Message

Before you hit the dance floor, JoJo has something to tell you. Crack the code to uncover her good luck message.

See answer on page 31.

Fav Routine

Is there a dance routine you just love? Fill in the steps here. Let the moves inspire you!

STEP 1	STEP 2	STEP 3	STEP 4

STEP 5	STEP 6	STEP 7	STEP 8

STEP 9	STEP 10	STEP 11	STEP 12

STEP 13	STEP 14	STEP 15	STEP 16

STEP 17	STEP 18	STEP 19	STEP 20

YOUR ROUTINE

It's time for you to be the choreographer.
Draw in the steps and try them out.
Don't forget the big finish!

DID YOU KNOW DANCE CAN BE PERFORMED FREESTYLE? THAT MEANS THERE ARE NO STEPS TO FOLLOW. LET THE MUSIC OR YOUR FEELINGS GUIDE YOU!

STEP 1	STEP 2	STEP 3	STEP 4

STEP 5	STEP 6	STEP 7	STEP 8

STEP 9	STEP 10	STEP 11	STEP 12

STEP 13	STEP 14	STEP 15	STEP 16

STEP 17	STEP 18	STEP 19	STEP 20

DON'T BE LATE!

JoJo's schedule is packed, but there's always time to dance. Help JoJo dance her way to rehearsal.

END

START

See answer on page 31.

DANCE SEQUENCE

Figure out which dance move completes each sequence.

See answers on page 31.

Dance Goals

It took years of hard work and practice for JoJo to become the dancer she is today. Write down your dance goals to become the best dancer you can be!

DID YOU KNOW JOJO TOOK HER FIRST DANCE CLASS WHEN SHE WAS 5 YEARS OLD?

Turns

....

....

Jumps

....

....

Stretches

....

....

Footwork

....

....

Performance

....

....

Poses

....

....

Rhythm

....

....

Expressions

....

....

Other

....

....

Other

....

....

DESIGNING DANCERS

You can't kick, slide, or spin to the beat without sweet sneakers on your feet. Draw your own designs to create fabulous new shoes.

WORK IT OUT

Feeling jittery before a competition or practice?
Work through your nerves with this relaxing coloring page.

Dance Terms

From dance moves to stage terms, how many of these words do you know?

BALL CHANGE

A dance step performed by shifting weight from the ball of one foot to the other, and back again.

CENTER STAGE

The middle of a stage, or the most prominent position to the audience.

DID YOU KNOW THAT JO PERFORMED HER FIRST SO TO "MAMA, I'M A BIG G NOW" FROM THE MUSIC *HAIRSPRAY*?

CHASSÉ

A dance step, a sliding step where one foot catches up to and moves the other. It is also known as a "step-together step."

CHOREOGRAPHY

The sequence of movements in a dance or the art of creating a dance.

EN POINTE

A dance position in which the dancer stands on the tips of their toes, often with special shoes.

DOWNSTAGE / UPSTAGE

The front of the stage closest to the audience (downstage), and the back of the stage farthest from the audience (upstage).

ENCORE

An additional performance at th end of a show, often demanded by the audience. It means "again" in French.

FLOOR WORK

..e movements performed
. the floor during a dance
..utine, or at the beginning
of a class as a warm-up.

FOOTWORK

The movement and
position of the feet
in dance.

ISOLATION

Moving one part of the
body, like the head or
hips, without moving
the other parts.

JETÉ

A dance step
performed by
leaping from one
foot to the other.

NAE NAE

A popular dance move
performed by shifting
weight from one foot to
the other with one
arm raised.

PARTNERING

When two dancers pair
up and perform
coordinated steps.

PIROUETTE

A dance step, a turn or
..pin performed on one
..eg with the other leg
bent at the knee.

PLIÉ

A dance step
performed by
bending the knees.

POPPING AND LOCKING

Types of hip-hop movements
often paired together. Popping
involves moving your body
outward, while locking involves
moving your body inward or
freezing your body in
a pose momentarily.

RELEVÉ

A dance step
..erformed by raising
..our heels so you are
standing on
your toes.

SOLO

A performance by
a single person, as
opposed to a group.

SPOTTING

When a dancer focuses
her eyesight on one
spot during a turn to
prevent dizziness.

STAGE LEFT / STAGE RIGHT

The sides of the stage from
the performers' point of
view looking at the audience.

Dance Terms Crossword

How many dance terms did you learn on the previous pages? Complete this crossword to show off your knowledge!

ACROSS
3. A turn or spin
5. Moving one part of your body
7. "Again" in French
8. A performance by a single person

DOWN
1. A leap from one leg to the other
2. The front of the stage closest to the audience
3. A bending of the knees
4. The movement and position of the feet
6. A type of hip-hop move that involves freezing

See answers on page 31.

Style Search

Find these styles of dance in the grid below. They may be hidden across, up and down, or diagonally.

BALLET   JAZZ   TAP

BALLROOM   LYRICAL   THEATRICAL

FOLK   MODERN

FREESTYLE   STEP

W	B	C	X	R	D	L	E	K	M	P	Q
X	F	R	E	E	S	T	Y	L	E	O	B
T	A	O	F	M	U	N	A	X	S	D	A
W	Z	B	W	I	T	W	D	A	T	K	L
I	T	K	A	B	M	K	E	R	E	U	L
N	L	A	W	L	Z	W	L	B	P	S	R
R	Q	W	P	Z	L	X	R	O	T	G	O
E	W	T	A	Y	I	E	A	J	F	M	O
D	Z	J	R	P	O	V	T	Y	L	E	M
O	T	L	A	C	I	R	Y	L	G	L	E
M	L	U	T	F	Y	I	P	Z	H	J	P
D	L	A	C	I	R	T	A	E	H	T	I

See answers on page 31.

Types of Dance

Have you ever heard someone mention a style of dance and wondered exactly what it was? Read JoJo's dance dictionary to learn about many different types of dancing!

Did You Know JoJo's favorite dance styles are jazz and hip-hop?

BALLET

A classical, theatrical style of dance which often tells a story. It is often performed in pointe shoes and focuses on a series of formal steps and poses for the arms and legs.

BALLROOM

Partner dancing where the couple rotates counterclockwise in a series of formal steps. It includes styles like the waltz, tango, East Coast swing, foxtrot, and samba.

JAZZ

A modern, theatrical dance form that focuses on isolated movements and a unique style.

HIP-HOP

A street dance style that includes breaking, popping, and locking. It can be performed freestyle, which means there is no choreography.

LYRICAL

A combination of jazz and ballet, often performed to songs with lyrics. It seeks to express the emotions of the song.

MODERN

A form of dance originally created in opposition to ballet. Flexed feet, clenched hands, and choreographed falls were introduced to show emotions that were unseen in previous kinds of dance.

STEP

Any style of dance that focuses on sounds created by the feet, like Irish step dance, clogging, or tap. Stepping, or step dancing, is an example that includes body percussion like clapping and the use of voice.

TAP

A theatrical dance in which the dancers wear special shoes with heel and toe taps that allow them to make a sound with every step they take. Performing tap steps without tap shoes is called "soft-shoe."

FOLK

A cultural dance passed down from generation to generation. Folk dances are unique to their region and can include any style of dance. They can be performed in front of an audience or danced by attendees at a gathering to celebrate an event, like a festival or a wedding.

THEATRICAL

Any style of dance performed onstage for an audience often with choreography, costumes, sets, and lighting. It is also known as "concert dance."

A Month of Dance Challenges

Keep your dancing fresh! Draw the icons on the dates below to plan a month of dance challenges.

Watch a Dance Video =

Dance Like Nobody's Watching =

Share a Dance =

Do Your Favorite Move =

Do a JoJo Move =

Try a New Style =

1		
2	3	4
5	6	7
8	9	10
11	12	13

DRESSED FOR SUCCESS

JoJo doesn't just dance—she dances in style! Add some color and patterns to these outfits.

SHOWSTOPPER

Time for a new routine! Use the steps and styles you've learned to choreograph some awesome steps for you and your besties.

STEP 1	STEP 2	STEP 3	STEP 4

STEP 5	STEP 6	STEP 7	STEP 8

STEP 9	STEP 10	STEP 11	STEP 12

STEP 13	STEP 14	STEP 15	STEP 16

STEP 17	STEP 18	STEP 19	STEP 20

ANSWERS

Page 3: Dance Words

RAHRYHEPCOOG = CHOREOGRAPHY
LELABT = BALLET
ZAZJ = JAZZ
PAT = TAP
ORMNDE = MODERN
PO-HPHI = HIP-HOP
LALMBORO = BALLROOM
LOOS = SOLO
CRALILY = LYRICAL
SMICU = MUSIC

Page 7: Strike a Pose

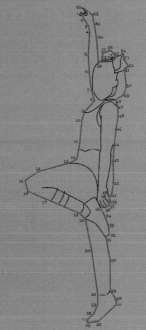

Page 10: Musical Notes

♪ *5*   ♫ *5*   ♩ *4*

4   *2*   *5*

4   ♪ *6*   *6*

6   ♪ *4*

Page 11: Secret Message

DANCE LIKE YOU MEAN IT

Page 14: Don't Be Late!

Page 15: Dance Sequence

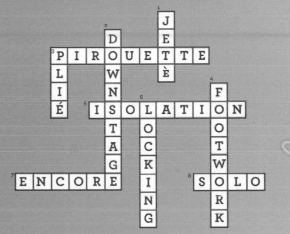

1. b   2. a   3. d   4. c

Page 22: Dance Terms Crossword

```
              J
        D     E
  P I R O U E T T E
  L     W     È
  I     N           F
  É     I S O L A T I O N
        T     O     O
        A     C     T
        G     K     W
  E N C O R E I   S O L O
        G     N     R
        I           K
        N
        G
```

Page 23: Style Search

W	B	C	X	R	D	L	E	K	M	P	Q
X	F	R	E	E	S	T	Y	L	E	O	B
T	A	O	F	M	U	N	A	X	S	D	A
W	Z	B	W	I	T	W	D	A	T	K	L
I	T	K	A	B	M	K	E	R	E	U	L
N	L	A	W	L	Z	W	L	B	P	S	R
R	Q	W	P	Z	L	X	R	O	T	G	O
E	W	T	A	Y	I	E	A	J	F	M	O
D	Z	J	R	P	O	V	T	Y	L	E	M
O	T	L	A	C	I	R	Y	L	G	L	E
M	L	U	T	F	Y	I	P	Z	H	J	P
D	L	A	C	I	R	T	A	E	H	T	I

31

Dance Dreams Card Game

Carefully pull out the cards at the back of this book to challenge yourself and your friends to up your dance game!

NUMBER OF PLAYERS: 1 to 5
MATERIALS: 30 playing cards (included), timer or clock that counts seconds
OBJECT: Have the most cards at the end of the game.

GAME PLAY:

ROUND ONE

SHUFFLE the cards and place the deck facedown in the middle of the players.
DRAW the cards. Starting with the youngest player and moving clockwise around the room, each player draws a card and assigns a dance move to the prompt on the card. The player shows the move and prompt to the group and adds the card to their hand. Repeat until each player has 5 cards in their hand.

Duplicate cards: There are two of each card in the deck. Only one move can be assigned to a dance prompt.

Freestyle cards: A unique move must be done each time a freestyle card is used in a routine.

PERFORM! Taking turns, each player gets 10 seconds to create a routine with their cards and memorize it. The player hands their cards off to another player and everyone counts the performer in with a "Five, six, seven, eight!"

Counting in: Once the performer is counted in, they cannot stop dancing! If the performer misses a move in their routine, that card goes into the discard pile. The performer keeps the card for each move they get right.

ROUNDS TWO and THREE

SHUFFLE the discard pile together with the rest of the deck.
DRAW the cards like in round one. Continue until the discard pile is empty.
PERFORM! Follow the same game play as round one. Players must use all of their cards in their routines. The player with the most cards at the end of round three wins.

Tiebreaker: If multiple players have the same number of cards at the end, they perform a speed round. Time each tied player as they perform their routines from round three. The performer who correctly performs their routine the fastest wins.

Alternate: For a single-player game or for longer game play with multiple players, repeat round three until no cards are left in the discard pile.

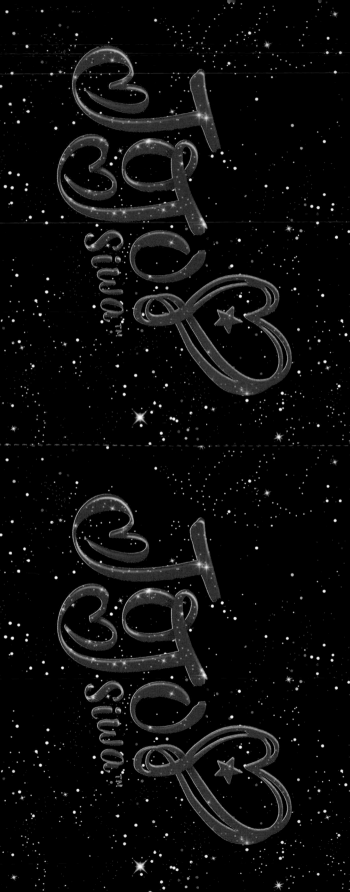

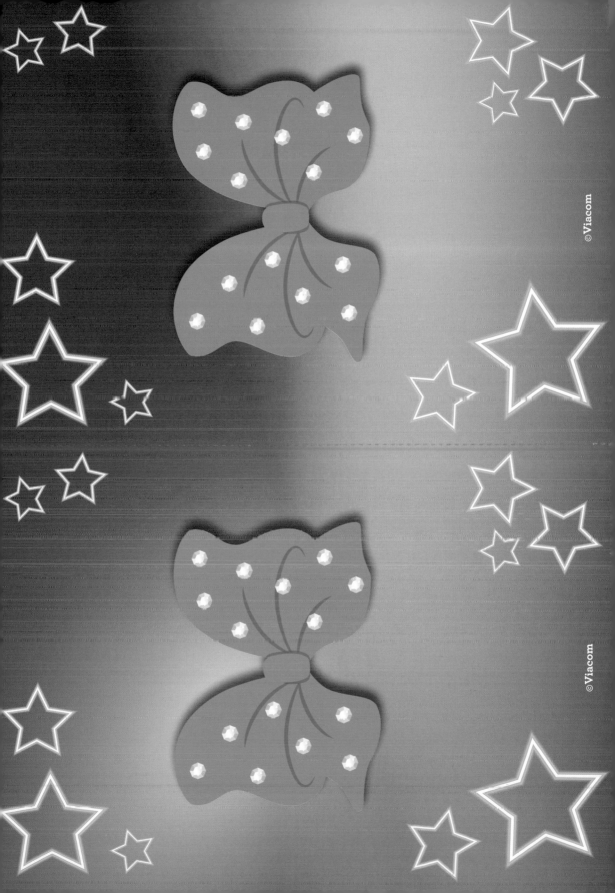